The Flirting MANUAL

Learning to Seduce the Most Beautiful Women

TIAGO PEREIRA

WORKBOOK PRESS LLC
187 E Warm Springs Rd,
Suite B285 Las Vegas NV 89119 USA
Website: https://workbookpress.com/
Hotline: 1-888-818-4856
Email: admin@workbookpress.com

Ordering Information:
Quantity sales. Special discounts are available on quantity purchases by corporations, associations, and others. For details, contact the publisher at the address above.

ISBN-13:   978-1-960752-81-9 - Paperback Version
                  978-1-960752-80-2 - Digital Version

PUB. DATE: 08/22/2025

The Flirting MANUAL

Learning to Seduce the Most Beautiful Women

TIAGO PEREIRA

Table of Contents

Women Want to Be Loved

Introduction

If dating or starting a conversation is like a second language to you, then with this ebook, you should have a little more confidence. Sometimes a simple hello is enough, depending on who you're talking to, but things will go in your favor if you offer women something; this will spark immediate interest in you. But there are two more things that you can talk about that will make things more interesting. I will reveal them later in the book.

You can use it to have great and indifferent sex with different (and amazingly hot) women every day of the week. If you want to fall in love, I'll teach you this too, and how to do it in the proper manner.

If you develop an FA (Flirting Artist) mentality—something will happen if you follow the advice on these pages—you will be practically immune to the growth of the pathetic and desperate fixations normally associated with falling in love. Indeed, this can happen—but its secondary effects (jealousy, depression, etc.) will be much less severe.

These negative things will have no room to develop or won't have enough time to reach their full potential.

The word polygamy is probably the most accurate way to describe how a seducer works at the level of love. He loves, but many women at the same time. Being in love with one woman at a time, especially if the feeling is one-sided, becomes a fixation.

He begins to show signs of despair, his ability to think clearly paralyzes, and there is the constant fear of being rejected.

When your feelings aren't corresponded, or when you aren't reciprocated the way you expect, your ego begins to decline, further repelling women in a vicious circle that just gets worse.

Being in love with many women at the same time (or at least being interested in many women at the same time, since they haven't yet given you enough reasons to reward them with your love) allows you to think with consistency and confidence.

You realize there are countless wonderful women, so you're relaxed enough to guide their feelings toward you. In addition, your confidence and unconcern attract more women, forming another cycle of feelings—but this time, a positive cycle for your self-esteem. These steps are about choices, about giving you the wisdom you need to explore all paths before deciding which one is right for you.

It doesn't matter if you seduce many women simultaneously, if you fall in love and get married, or if you become a monk who leads a celibate life. Just be sure that whatever you choose, do it in the fullness of your wisdom and with your eyes wide open.

ONE

Which One Are You?

FA (Flirting Artist)

He is an adult who has mastered the art of flirting, romance, and satisfying beautiful women. His characteristics include a huge dose of self-confidence, a good-looking appearance, and a high success rate in sexual situations. The FA understands that all situations involving attractive women are passionate.

CFS (Common Frustrated Sucker)

This is a commonly used term to describe a healthy, excited adult male who has never stopped long enough to meditate about what women want and need. Therefore, he will not have the slightest chance to even try to be successful in seducing and satisfying a woman.

TWO

The Ten Rules of Seduction

If you follow these ten rules, you'll be amazed at how successful you can be.

1. Always Be in Control

Here are the most frequently asked questions:

What is the most important aspect of being a successful seduction artist?

What is the one crucial difference between a CFS addicted to masturbation and a sexually satisfied FA? The answer is simple: control.

FAs are always in control of the situation. The CFSs let other things—the woman, the other man, or their emotions—dictate how they will act and what they will achieve in the end.

If you want to have success with women, the first thing you must do is control yourself. You can't afford to be nervous or panicked in a situation of seduction. You have to remain calm and confident in all situations. And you should always exude an image of calm and confidence.

Never put too much pressure on yourself, never worry about being rejected, and, as the old saying goes, never let them see you sweat.

The second thing that you must control is the situation itself. Seduction should advance according to the rhythm you have defined, which means you should always be close to the woman, just like the conversation that you initiate. Act quickly, knowing exactly what you want, and you will be on the right path to a successful seduction.

The third thing you need to control is the woman. But for God's sake, don't be intimidating., And don't act macho.

Control has to do with subtly taking the woman to the place where you want her to be (excited and totally yours) and then leaving her there. Women want a man who is confident and powerful.

Show her that you're a dominant male, and she will instinctively follow the path traced by you. But remember, with great power comes great responsibility. Always listen to her and show respect. And if you promise her the best time of her life, you should keep that promise.

The fourth thing that you have to control is the relationship. Never pay for a woman's drinks or dinner. Never let her cancel a date or treat you badly. Always make yourself aware that you're prepared to end it all, and she will crawl back to you.

Easier said than done, right? Control is easy to obtain, since this possibility depends on you.

You already have the power. And provided you have the right attitude, the exact techniques, and the right guide (such as in these pages), it's impossible for you to be defeated.

Remember the Following Essentials

- Never be nervous.
- Don't panic!
- Never worry about being rejected.
- Always be in control of the situation.
- Don't be intimidating.
- Never pay for drinks or dinner before going to bed with them.
- Always be prepared to end everything right away.

2. Be the Alpha Male

If you usually watch Discovery or National Geographic channels, you are aware of the dominant alpha-male concept. The dominant male is the leader. He is the master recognized by the rest of the animals in his pack. He's the one the females surround themselves with and males respect.

He's the one who has sex all the time, while the other males hope he disappears so their opportunity appears. The chances are minimal unless one of them becomes the next leader, which takes us back to square one: you still need to be the dominant alpha male.

When it comes to people the dominant male isn't necessarily the strongest or the most beautiful male of the group. The dominant male is simply the one who has sex. Do females want this male? Yes, because he's the dominant one, of course.

This is a prophecy that can be fulfilled in itself. Project an image of a dominant male, and you'll have the females all around you. Once he goes to bed with all females, he is, by definition, the dominant male.

The first step is the most difficult one. After that, everything gets easier—and better. You need to show the woman you're the dominant man, and she'll kneel on her own.

The secret is this: women instinctively love powerful men. The key word is, of course, instinctively. Even the most beautiful woman, the one full of attitude, who seems so proud and in charge of the situation, wants to surrender (at least for one night) to a man with sexual power.

This attitude is merely a facade to keep the submissive men away. She doesn't want someone even weaker than she is. She wants someone to protect her and give her everything she deserves. She can sometimes dominate the conversation and dominate him in bed (and I'm completely in favor of it!), but she still wishes to respect him in the morning.

So what's the first step in becoming a dominant male? How do you become a man who goes to bed with everyone before you even get to bed? It's easy. You simply have to project the image of a dominant male and believe women want to be with you.

What really matters is that you can't fake it. You really have to believe you are the best man for this woman. Transform yourself, and it will transform your reality. Doubt yourself, and you're preparing for failure.

The easiest way to convert yourself from a submissive loser into a winner is to determine which dominant male model you should be. Then you just have to become that model.

Again, none of this has anything to do with force, appearance, or money, so don't imagine yourself physically different from what you are. Instead, imagine yourself as the following:

- confident, since you're a dominant male;
- profligate, to a certain extent;
- rightful, because you know people are watching you;
- courteous, because you know your stature is based on satisfying women; and
- good company, because you know that, in the end, the woman will choose you instead of the submissive male even if he is soft-spoken and gives you a good mouthful.

Watch Out!

In human communities, there's more than one dominant alpha male. Unlike a group of lions or seals, we don't have to fight for eight or ten females; we have millions of women at our disposal from which we can choose.

This means you don't have to worry that someone with more muscles or full of gentle conversations will invade your territory. But sometimes it may mean you may have to fight for this one.

You don't have to be the biggest stallion in the room, and generally you'll never have to fight to prove you're a man. All you have to do to have sex is to detach yourself from the pathetic heap of men. That's not so hard, is it? A good FA doesn't care about other dominant males; Women are the ones you need to focus your eyes on.

3. Always Be Your Best.

To meet women, you have to be prepared physically and emotionally. You have to feel good about yourself, and I don't just say confident. I mean other aspects as well. The first step toward feeling confident is to always be your best on all levels.

CFSs have a problem with their appearance. They worry about being small, bald, or fat or having acne, and they let it affect their posture, facial expressions, and body language.

I've said it many times. It isn't only the physical aspect that counts. It isn't because you're bald that women do not get excited by you. Your lack of confidence is why this happens.

What matters is how you feel about yourself because women pick up on your attitude and use it against you. If you approach a woman with an attitude that isn't really interesting to her, she'll convince herself that it's true. Project an extremely successful image—that she's lucky to have an opportunity to meet you—even if she may initially feel skeptical.

Never worry about things you cannot change (no, plastic surgery on your nose doesn't count). Pay close attention to those things you can change. Your clothes should always be clean and fit perfectly. Your hair should be well styled. Your teeth should be clean, and fresh breath is important, and, of course, you should be freshly bathed.

Never undervalue an outlet, even if it's the supermarket to buy a pack of beer. As you will later learn in this book, people meet at the strangest places, and the most accidental encounters can lead to the most rewarding relationships—if you're prepared to seize the opportunity, of course. There's no right or wrong way to dress to impress women, but the clothes you wear are a mirror of who and what you are, so be careful. An Armani suit is beautiful, but it gives women the impression that you are a spendthrift who will buy her things, when you aren't! A fashion-oriented look makes you stand out, but some women will not take you seriously because it makes them feel square, and that affects their confidence.

The worst mistake you can make is presenting yourself as a classic swinger, sporting an open collar and large gold chains. No woman likes you to toy with her, so don't advertise through your outfit that you're a joker. This closes the door before it even opens. And for God's sake, never consult these tips in front of a woman. Women don't like things studied and rehearsed; they want spontaneity (or something that seems spontaneous). That's why typical pickup phrases rarely work. If you don't really have a personal style, your best bet is the "casual look." Go from khakis to black designer pants. Throw out your golf polo and buy a shirt. Prefer a "conservative" hairstyle, but one in the style of a reputable hairdresser, not a barber.

This way of dressing may not open many doors, but it also won't get you hit in the face with one. Remember: it isn't the clothes that make the man, it's the way you use them.

Look after Your Appearance
- wear clean, well-fitting clothes;
- take a shower;
- brush your teeth and hair;
- select your clothes carefully;
- comb yourself without exaggeration;
- use a perfume that isn't too strong; and
- be confident.

4. Be Confident

Trust is the quality that most needs to be developed by a dominant male. Confidence means feeling comfortable when you approach any woman at any time, since even before meeting her you already know you're the best thing that can happen to her.

Dominant men never question whether they are good enough for a woman; they ask themselves if the woman is good enough for them. They never offer anything to a woman. They never sell themselves; they try to learn what a woman can offer them.

Now that you're aware of the concept of trust—forget everything you've ever heard about this word. If you're not feeling confident, it's because you lack confidence in yourself; you're nervous and need self-assurance.

If you're truly a dominant male, you feel so positive about a sexual encounter that the word trust will never enter your mind. Feeling so naturally relaxed so that you never think of the word trust is the most trusting act of all. Focus on feeling relaxed and positive, and you will project a tremendous sense of confidence.

If you need a small incentive to approach a beautiful woman, don't tell yourself to be confident, be confident. Instead, repeat this mantra: "I am the best thing that ever happened to this woman."

Think about the chills she'll feel and the way you make her feel inside, and, if you want, imagine for a second all the ways you can make her achieve orgasm. However, don't dwell on this thought. Advance, and give yourself the best experience of your life.

5. Have the Right Mental Disposition

If you've ever been to a nightclub, you've noticed those men sitting or standing around the dance floor, looking at the women dancing but not taking any real action, waiting for something to happen.

Their mental disposition is, *If I stay around long enough, maybe something will happen*. This is not good! And I'm not just talking about one evening at nightclubs. I'm talking about your daily life also.

Do you realize all the beautiful women who pass you every day? Do you make any kind of eye contact with them? Do you try to do anything more than stare at their buttocks when they're not realizing? Do you deviate your eyes when they try to look at you?

Some men call this being "reserved," others call it being afraid; either way, it's not right. If you don't take advantage of every minute of your day when you're surrounded by beautiful women, then you're no better than those people around the dance floor. Like them, you go home alone and remember all the beautiful women you've seen, and you fall asleep alone.

If you're at a nightclub, the obvious answer is to go to the dance floor. Before you take this step, remember that you're about to meet a beautiful woman—so get ready to do something more than just standing there looking at her b*** or her boobs in the hope of not getting caught in the act.

6. Follow the Three-Second Rule

There's one rule to remember, and with all honesty, this may be the most important one I'll teach you. It's an old FA secret called the three-second rule," or simply 3S.

The 3S is as follows: Once the woman is found, you have three seconds to make your "move." If you hesitate … forget it. Forget her and head to the next available female.

Even if you don't remember anything to start a conversation, never break the three-second rule. You have to get noticed and make a good first impression.

When you use the 3S—you don't just use it, you follow it—it shows that you aren't afraid. You're taking the initiative and coming down from your pedestal, and this can only work in your favor.

If you don't follow the 3S, you're in a decidedly weaker position. First, it will not look strong or spontaneous. On the contrary, if you establish too much eye contact or simply hesitate, you'll appear weak and unsure.

Instead of talking to her, you're giving this woman time to form an opinion about you, and she's thinking you're just like the others: afraid to take the first step.

However, you aren't doing yourself a favor for waiting. When you hesitate, you're giving yourself time to feel intimidated and make excuses about why you aren't approaching this woman.

This is the other advantage of 3S: it doesn't give you an opportunity to rethink the situation. You don't have time to sweat, tremble, and stammer. In other words, you don't have time to get the typical symptoms of a classic CFS. It's guaranteed that if you're new to these ideas, or if the woman is really beautiful, you may stutter and sweat during the conversation, but at least half the distance has already been traveled.

When you make a good first impression— it will remain in her mind long after your conversation. Also, if you approach with your best foot forward, you're much less likely to become a bowl of gelatin during the conversation.

And don't worry: after practicing the 3S rule, you'll think of a great approach every time you talk to a woman for the first time.

7. Never Be a Nice Guy

The debate about being a good boy or a fool is one of the oldest battles in the sexual universe. The good guys are polite, caring, friendly, sweet, tender, and romantic. This kind of man has a tendency to have many friends but not many lovers and may even spend a whole night talking to a beautiful woman, but letting her escape into the arms of a bad guy. They barely leave a woman's side except to use the bathroom.

We have to face the truth: it's those people who get the women. Due to this, most people assume that seduction advices (such as these) will teach men to be bad. And you know what? It's somewhat true.

The problem is that most people—or should I say the people who don't understand the rules of the game—have wrong definitions of "good guys" and "bad guys."

They think a bad guy is a convincing, aggressive, rude, narcissistic, and muscular man who's always predisposed to having sex and doesn't care about the women he sleeps with. This isn't entirely true …

However, I have to admit that nine out of ten men that I just described will be the ones who take the woman to their beds, while the good guys are left out in the rain holding a bouquet of flowers.

Why? It's not that women like to have sex with bad guys. Women prefer education over rudeness and attention over distraction. The problem is how the nice guys demonstrate their positive characteristics. In order to appear friendly and romantic, these "good guys" think they need to turn off their sexuality. They hide their desires to not offend women, demonstrating an androgynous or asexual personality. The first impression they give is one of effeminacy, weakness, and lack of sexual desire.

At best, they confuse women who question whether these guys even find them appealing. At worst, women lose all respect for them. Is it necessary for me to tell you that this is a huge mistake. Women have to know you desire them, so make them feel that they're on solid ground, and dispel any doubt about the possibility of not granting their desires.

In order to make this clear, you'll have to internalize your sexual desires and feel comfortable with sexual issues. Is it wrong to let a woman realize that you find her attractive and sexually stimulating? Is it rude to be honest about the fact that, like everyone else on the planet, you appreciate sex?

This is what the bad guys offer to women and that the good guys don't: they aren't afraid to be sexual. It's your sexuality that attracts women, because women are also sexual beings, and they want to be with someone with enough confidence to satisfy their desires.

So go ahead and be well-mannered, kind, romantic, and friendly with women—all these are characteristics that you will learn to use and internalize in this book. But never—I said never—forget to let her know that you want her sexually.

Take Care!
- Never lie!
- If you promise to give her a call, give her a call!

Things You Should Never Do to a Woman!

An FA is only considered an bad guy by two types of people: the men who steal the women, and the women who think he lied to them and treated them like trash. Forget these men. They're losers. But always be careful about your reputation with women.

Never lie to them. If you're only interested in a one-night stand, make it clear. If you have several women at the same time, clue her in before you let her jump into your bed. And if you tell a woman you'll call to her, always do so. No exceptions.

8.   Never Go on a "Night Out"!

By now some of you might be thinking, *Wow, wouldn't it be great to go out with a beautiful woman—a woman who respects me, wants me, and cannot take her eyes off me?* Give yourself some time, dude.

If you want to be a successful FA, or even just want to conquer the woman of your dreams, forget that romantic image of candlelight dinner—at least in the near future.

There are zillions of better ways to meet a woman: playing sports together, renting a movie, and meeting up for coffee. But never call it "dating," and always make it an issue for her to pay for what she eats and drinks. If she refuses to pay, do something different and take a walk with her; maybe she was interested in doing something different. Is there a right time to go out on a date with a woman? Actually, yes. Encounters are exclusive privileges and rewards for women with whom you sleep. End of story.

What's the worst thing you can do to a woman? Offer to pay for her drink. This just sends the worst possible message: despair, misunderstanding, lack of power—not to mention that it's the worst cliché in the world. If I've said it once, I'll say it hundreds more times: never spend a single dollar on a woman until she deserves it.

9. Learn to Love Rejection

I've never been rejected. I only found out if a woman has good taste or not!
—Author and TV personality Ross Jeffries

The truth is, once the solutions to these issues have been put to work, men will never be rejected again. Why? Because you will never use a bad pickup line again, make an offer to dance from out of nowhere, or give any other obvious opening, only to get her rejection. And once in the cockpit, you'll be able to read the signs and get out of the way before she dumps you.

However, in the early days, and even at a later stage of its development, you will receive rejections. Don't take them personally. Just because she doesn't want it now doesn't mean the same thing will happen in the future. Maybe you haven't tried hard enough. Maybe your approach was wrong. Maybe she had a bad day. Maybe she has a boyfriend and doesn't want to give you the chance to persuade her to betray him. Maybe she'll come back after a few hours or on another night.

If she doesn't come back, who cares? After all, she's going to miss an excellent experience. You were about to give her a good gift, and she refused it. Poor thing.

In truth, even the best FAs lose more than they win. Did you even wonder what it's like to have a 50 percent statistic? That would mean that each time you approached two women, one would end up sleeping with you! Believe me, it won't happen. This event can take place for a week, a month, or even an entire summer, but in the end, it will be difficult to maintain that rhythm.

The key to being an FA relies on the ability to deal with rejection. You cannot let a bad date bring you down or destroy your confidence. Instead, think of rejection as a positive thing. Whenever you're rejected, you learn something. In other words, every time a woman refuses you, you might have been close to having sex with her.

After all, if you don't try, nothing will happen, so keep trying and never give too much importance to the victories or the losses. Never play the smart guy if the woman accepts your advances. It's just sex. Another big date doesn't mean you're a winner for the rest of your life. But never get too down when a woman rejects you. You aren't a loser because some women don't want to sleep with you—they're the ones who are losing out.

Don't misunderstand what I'm saying. This isn't easy. For most people, the most difficult part is the transition from a CFS to an FA.

The next section is filled with practical advice on how to face and ignore the insults you will receive.

Once you can handle rejection, everything begins to fit in: your confidence, your mental readiness, and your attitude. When you can deal with rejection with style and class, you will become a dominant (alpha) male.

The Three Rules for Rejection

There are only three reasons to be rejected by a woman:
- 1—A Boyfriend or Husband

If she's monogamous, this has nothing to do with you.
- 2—She Wants Your FA Friend

Your friend is an FA, so you don't have reason to be ashamed.
- 3—She Isn't Confident Enough to Say Yes

Believe it or not, many women automatically reject men because they don't feel good enough to say yes (this is their problem, not yours).

Remember these three points, and they'll help you maintain your confidence.

Remember: she's the one who's losing.

10. There Will Always Be Another Woman

I know many of you probably bought this book to finally learn how to start a conversation with that dream woman you see every day at the cafe. Well, I have news for you: you will never have it—at least not this way.

The problem is, you have the wrong attitude. If a woman is your only project—the one you think about day and night, imagining different scenarios for an approach, and desperately trying to make her like you—this is called despair.

This will be noticed. She'll understand this, consciously or unconsciously, and there's nothing worse for putting off a woman than a desperate man. When you let yourself fall into the trap of obsession, you begin to overanalyze everything the woman of your dreams does, every step she takes, everything she says—and then you relate all that to yourself. What's the result? Confusion, frustration, and anxiety. Your confidence is gone—just like any chance of giving her a positive and comfortable image of yourself.

Yes, your obsession is going to drive you mad, but the effect on her is even worse. If she feels you're obsessed with her, she knows you've been analyzing her every move.

At best, this will make her cautious when she's near you. At worst, it will scare her immensely, and she'll do anything to stay away from you.

But wait: maybe the attraction is mutual. Perhaps by showing her that you're obsessed with her—but that you aren't man enough to approach her—she'll give you a positive signal that will relieve the pressure and ensure your success. If it's too obvious, maybe she'll approach you first.

Do not think this way! Remember the 3S Rule. And never leave the ball in the women's court. You have to control the situation, or you won't have any chance of success. This is the number-one rule of the FA.

Second, if she gives you a signal, will you be able to see it? Most likely you won't even notice a signal, or you'll have doubts about the reality of it, and once again you'll convince yourself that you won't talk to her ...

If you're obsessed with a woman, if you want her so badly that you can't handle the idea that you can be rejected (a definitive CFS), there's only one thing to do: meet at least ten other women. Once this is done, the obsession will calm down and you'll feel more relaxed when you're around her.

If this is your first love, or if she's the reason you bought this book, you have to meet other women! This will give you the confidence to approach the woman of your dreams from the right angle, with the right attitude. Remember, when it comes to women, trust is everything.

And who knows if, even after meeting twenty women, you'll realize she isn't all that you want in your life. But, if she's still the woman of your dreams, congratulations. With my counsel and your experience, she will be yours.

But, first of all, you have to meet twenty other women, so you'd better start learning how to meet these women.

THREE

The Truth about Women

The first myth about women is that they have to be totally on their own, and they want it so badly they'll go out with you. Obviously this is setting a very high bar, but the good news is that this is totally untrue. In fact, a woman will accept your advances (without giving herself in full) as long as she finds you relatively attractive, confident and, most importantly, interesting.

Many single women are lonely. That is a fact. Men often approach women with the pretense of asking them out, but for some reason they don't have the courage to follow through. This is even more true when it comes to especially beautiful women. When dominant males (you) actually have the confidence to invite these women out for a romantic evening, most women will accept, even if he isn't her prince charming (for now).

The second myth tells us that women are not looking for men—or sex. Of course they are! Women love romance; they want someone to kiss, hug, and go to the movies with; they long to walk in the clouds.

However, they're also cautious, so never let the first impression deter you. There are many women who intentionally pass an image of being unattainable, leaving a vibration of "leave me alone or I'll tear your head off" in the air as a form of protection against a shattered heart.

It's also the most correct way to remove all the CFS who have no idea how to approach a woman and fear even the simplest of challenges.

Don't worry. In most cases, this attitude is a simple and thin shield. If you approach it with confidence and refuse to take no for an answer, your persistence will bring dividends.

Always remember that getting close to a woman is the most

important part of any kind of seduction, and behind that hard wall is a romantic and soft heart. Break that barrier, and you're halfway to the finish line. The key to overcoming this line is to direct her thoughts toward sex.

In a good seduction, an innocent conversation will slowly lead her to think about you as a possible partner rather than just another cool guy. You're planting this idea in her head; it's leading her to think about you in a different way.

Did it ever happen where you had a woman interested in you, and suddenly you found yourself fonder of her than before? Well, that's basically what you're doing during seduction. When you put yourself in her thoughts, ones diverted toward sex, you're giving yourself a chance.

The point of a seduction isn't to take a woman straight to bed. This will happen—and I'm going to teach you how to run into those women—but in most cases, you'll end the meeting by asking for her phone number.

Leaving at the right time is an essential part of keeping the fish on the hook, but there's another factor at stake: going out on a "date" (we'll talk later and in more detail on the concept of an encounter) with an unknown woman is quite exciting.

The atmosphere of "anything can happen" helps change a woman's mood. It makes her feel like she's throwing caution to the wind—and she's likely to do things she normally wouldn't.

FOUR

The Hot Women and Only the Hot Ones

Whatever the circumstances—and no excuses for still being a beginner—always approach the most beautiful woman wherever you are. This is a short, quick rule that should never be missed. You can always decrease the quality of the woman of your choosing, but you'll miss out on the beautiful ones.

This may sound intimidating—as in, "Why would any beautiful woman want to be with me?" But stop and think. What do you hope to achieve by approaching a less beautiful one? Do you think she'll be more receptive because she's less wanted? Do you think she'll accept your advances out of desperation? Or does all this have to do with your level of comfort and self-esteem?

Whatever your arguments may be, I can assure you you're wrong. First, you're good enough for any woman, and if you don't believe it, then you're losing out. It has nothing to do with physical appearance or money. You're the man who can give her what she wants: fun.

Second, attractive women are no harder to hook than ugly ones. The fact is, all women love romance and want to feel special, and few women are satisfied with what they have.

Beautiful women get a lot of attention, but they're rarely asked out on dates because they intimidate men. In other words, if she seems unapproachable, it's most likely because everyone else thinks the same way. Opportunity is calling you.

FIVE

Talk to Women Everywhere

You're new to this, and a little intimidated by beautiful women, but no problem. No one goes from CFS to FA overnight; you have to evolve, just like that first single- celled organism that came out of the water and began to breathe the sweet air of life.

The most important thing that will make moving from a hard-pressed and stuttering CFS to a confident and sophisticated FA is experience. I can name hundreds of important rules and tips, but it all comes down to intuition. And it only appears—care to guess?—when you interact with women.

If you want to be a playboy, you have to develop your self-confidence as well as an intuitive sense for what women feel. This is done by talking to them all the time: in city parks, on buses, or at McDonald's, the supermarket, car washes, bowling alleys, airports, and laundromats. Everywhere you see beautiful women, be prepared to make your move.

In fact, until being an experienced FA with numerous accomplishments, you should speak with at least fifty new women per week. And remember, this is a minimum! Of course, if you go from zero to fifty, the transition can be a bit harsh, so go ahead and leave some free hours in the late afternoon or on Saturday afternoons to talk exclusively to all the women you see.

That's right: when I say all women, I mean all women, no matter how intimidating they seem or how strange the situation may be. If you do not force yourself to do it, you will never learn—and you will never have sex.

Do you need a little more follow up? Don't worry. I'll guide you step by step from your unlucky single status to your evolution as an experienced seducer (or at least a conversationalist) by the end of this chapter. But for now, let's review some extremely important basics.

Signs of Interest

I don't believe in signs of interest. If a woman isn't momentarily interested, it only means she has some work ahead of her to make her care about you later. The only thing that really matters is whether you're interested in her.

However, I understand that this attitude takes some time to develop. So for all you beginners, here's a list of tips, I found, that will teach you to read the mind of a woman who's on the other side of the room.

She's Interested

- She looks at you from the corner of her eye;
- She looks at you and then looks away several times;
- She quickly looks into your eyes;
- She looks away after a short look down;
- She changes her position;
- She touches her hair or clothing;
- She turns your body toward you;
- She slightly closes her eyes;
- She smiles;
- She imitates your posture.

She's Not Interested

- She doesn't even sneak a glance at you;
- She only establishes quick eye contact;
- She quickly looks away;
- She turns her eyes away, keeping her eyes at the same level;
- She doesn't change posture;
- She doesn't make any adjustments;
- She diverts her body from your direction;
- She doesn't smile;
- She doesn't mimic your posture;
- Her eyes don't move at all;
- She shrugs.

SIX

Capitalize

Sometimes, a woman cares about you because you're a smart, well built, confident, dominant male. It could be a coworker, neighbor, study partner, or even the woman in the shop where you go for your favorite coffee. It happens all the time.

If you have any feelings for her, don't let this window of opportunity close! She is preconditioned to like herself, so why should she let this chance slip through her fingers? At any minute, a new woman could catch your eye. Even without the threat of competition (who can be compared to you?), your interest can disappear without any logical reason.

Be careful not to do so in a suppliant way, which is foreign to the gender of the CFS. This is the main reason for the phenomenon, "I was interested in him until he became interested in me." Keep your posture haughty. Be confident.

A woman who has developed interest in you independently is no different from a woman you've just met. You have yet to realize that you're the man of her dreams using the techniques in this book. And if she's still interested, you'd better do it right now!

Don't wait for the nonexistent "right time" to approach her. And never expect her to take the first step—because she won't. She will eventually think you aren't interested, or worse, that you're too cowardly to go after what you want.

But what if she's not really interested? And if her signs of interest are just gestures of friendship or just your imagination at work? Now you're thinking like a CFS. Never disregard a woman's interest or be discouraged from approaching her. Believe me: if you noticed the signs, they're true.

SEVEN

The Myth of the Right Moment

It's not the right time yet, or the right moment.

By telling yourself this, you kill your dreams from coming to fruition. Life is too uncertain to wait around for the "right time." You have to get out of your comfort zone to evolve and go forward, because if you're not going forward then you're going backwards or being stagnant at best thus you're not using your time properly.

You have to replace fear with unshakable confidence, thinking and acting in positive ways and taking up challenges are a great way to defeat fear.

The primary purpose of seduction is to get the woman to reach a sexual frenzy, giving her the will to make love wherever she is. You aren't working based on her time but also on yours, and sometimes this says the right time is *now*.

Never send wrong messages/signs about your intentions. You do not want to look anxious, but in the end, your desire should never be put into doubt.

You're a man. You have sexual desires. It's not worth denying them. That should be exactly the attitude you should take. Your mantra is: "I'm a man."

EIGHT

Places to Meet Women

You're a beginner, and you're anxious. You have your house in order, your appearance is flawless, and your confidence is on the rise. You're a male ready to hunt, and you're prepared to venerate the 3S rule and soon pass into action. Now, you need to get some women, so it's time to go to the nearest bar or disco and—*not so fast, Romeo.* There are better places to meet women than under the pressure, volume, and amount of alcohol on a dance floor. Regardless of your level of fitness or ease—especially if you're a beginner—the following options are much more affordable for your wallet and your confidence than a bar or nightclub.

Malls

Malls are by far the best place to meet women. On one hand, there are beautiful women everywhere. On the other hand, they're normally on the move, which can easily lead to an encounter — This can be important for an amateur FA, not yet proficient in the art of dealing with and deflecting rejection. Take a look around the stores and look out for single or attractive customers. The products on the shelves will give you an excellent idea for getting started, the way you talk is crucial. Your job is to talk to her about those products.

If the mall is near an office complex, walk through the restaurant area during lunchtime. This place will be filled with women from the offices.

Coffee Shops

It's like visiting a bar but without alcohol, the loud music, and the constant good/bad vibe from your surroundings. Before work, at lunch, and in the late afternoon, these places are full of women, and this gives you the perfect opportunity to sit close to one and start a conversation. Libraries and Bookstores also. If there's a place where more women than men visit in larger numbers, it's libraries and bookstores. It's also the last place a woman expects to have a chat, so it's easy to catch them unawares. Before they realize what hit them, they're ready to take a break from all those boring books.

Self-Improvement Seminars

These classes are filled with beautiful and suggestible women who are seeking to expand their minds with new experiences and advice. Find out where they're taking place, and wait at the door for coffee, tea, and pee breaks.

Gyms

I put gyms almost at the bottom of the list because they can be intimidating, especially if you're not in good shape and lack confidence. This probably isn't the best option for beginners, but remember: women in the gym are hot. Yoga, tai chi, and other body/mind classes attract women who are generally in good shape, friendly, flexible, and open-minded. Can you think of a better combination?

Universities

These can also be intimidating places for beginners (particularly if you're older than twenty-five), but this is where college girls are. It's not worth saying any more. Nightclubs and Bars versus the Real World I just told you that you won't want to go to a bar or club to attract a woman. However, you may ask, aren't they filled with women? Is there much difference between a bar and a shopping center? The answer to these questions is yes, but the second is by far more important. There's really a huge difference between approaching a woman in a nightclub than in a mall: your expectations and mental disposition are different, women expect to hit on in nightclubs.

Remember that as a dominant male FA, you're always ready for a sexual encounter regardless of the environment you're in.

When you approach them in a mall, café, or a nontraditional place of engagement, you almost certainly catch them by surprise. I have found that this often works in your favor. She wasn't expecting attention, so she's especially pleased to have been noticed by you.

And once you've surprised her, she's more likely to think that your gesture was spontaneous and only about her. As such, she's much more inclined to give you her phone number, as well as to remember you fondly when you call her, even if you only had a brief conversation.

On the other hand, when she's "working" in a bar or club, the woman is already counting on being the target of masculine attention. In fact, if she's hot (and you would never target one that wasn't, right?), she must have been harassed at least a couple of times before you showed up.

Of course, this may work in your favor, since, thanks to this book, your approach technique will be much better than the pathetic pick up lines used by simpletons. Besides that, she can be in the bar or the club in search of some action. It's also for that reason that you're there. After all, women also know how to play this game.

However, on the whole, I find it much more pleasant and easier to surprise a woman than to try to impress her when she has her guard up. In a bar, the woman is psychologically prepared to walk away. On the street, she doesn't suspect that this can happen, and hence, outside approaches are usually better received. Besides that, the worst that can happen is that she will keep walking.

Personal Ads

For many beginners, personal ads seem like the perfect compromise — but it defeats the whole purpose of meeting women. This method is used by weak minds and weak people. You're practicing to be an FA, and if you choose to take a shortcut, you will never learn the techniques you need to win women on your own.

You will always be the boy with his face buried in the newspaper, with the immense fear of going out and talking to them, waiting and praying that some woman falls into your lap. This isn't a way to live your life. Besides, most of the women you'll meet through the ads are hideous.

Casual Dating

Women want to meet their prince charming in an accidental way, as if this could happen. They hate admitting to their friends that they met the prince in a bar or nightclub, and meeting men on the street is only a little better. They prefer meeting men at a private party (such as a birthday or a wedding), through a mutual friend, or through an event organized around an interest or hobby. It's much more romantic that way, and women love romance.

Blind dates are much easier, because instead of being in doubt, you come with the implicit recommendation of your friend or social group. You two already have something in common, so you already have something to talk about. And if you both have a friend in common, this will naturally clear up any doubt for her, such as whether you have a problem, or you don't like something she did, because misunderstandings can occur sometimes.

Of course, waiting to meet a woman in a casual situation will actually lessen your chances. That's why it's important to know some "approaches" — that there are women through whom you can meet other women. It's also a good idea to develop some hobbies. Yes, engaging women and having sex is an excellent hobby, but it's always a good idea to have other kinds of activities.

However, being an FA isn't an excuse to stop practicing your cool approach! Approaching women on the street is the best way to improve your experience and confidence, as these encounters are very difficult.

Have you ever heard the words "practice makes it perfect"? You're thinking, *Enough of this. I just want to go to bed with somebody tonight—I'm going to hunt the easier prey.*

Well, let me tell you something: practice makes perfection. While only a beginner, you constantly need to think about and work out your techniques so that you'll not only occasionally win the jackpot, you'll win big whenever you want.

When graduating from a CFS to an experienced FA, you'll savor the challenge and the novelty of new environments, and believe it or not, you'll reach a time when flirting is almost as fun as your evolution during the game.

So whatever your technical level is, it's always better to shake things up a bit. Casual encounters are easier, but coupling is more rewarding.

The choice is yours, but a healthy mix of the two is the woman's way of acting. When your confident approach is at its peak, a chance encounter is like a walk in the park.

In the next chapter, we start our beginner's course.

NINE

How to Start Feeling More Comfortable with Women

We've learned the basics, and now I'm starting at the beginning to guide you through the whole process until you're ready to engage a woman.

Believe me: if you've never talked to a strange woman before, the first step is not to go out there and try to hook a hottie. And, no, we will not practice with ugly ones either.

Instead, I will guide you through a series of steps that will teach you to talk to women in nonsexual situations. This relieves the pressure as well as the fear of rejection. I will not set any kind of time-out to follow these steps. Move at your own pace, but always give your maximum to move to the next level.

If you're sufficiently experienced (or confident) to pass these steps, go directly to the next section. The sooner you pass these beginner phases, the sooner you'll end up in bed with a woman.

Step 1—Visual Contact

To seduce a woman, you have to make her notice you. This is rule number one. (Rule number two tells us she wants you to notice her in a positive way.)

When you look a woman in the eye, she catches your eye, and you project an image of power. You aren't intimidated; you know what you want. It excites a woman.

The goal isn't to stare like an idiot but to stare at her as someone who knows what he's doing. The first way to look at her is frightening; to fix your eyes on her is a powerful thing.

Here's what you should do. Go to the mall and take a walk. When you see a beautiful woman coming toward you, wait until she's about ten feet away and start looking into her eyes. When she looks at you, try to maintain eye contact.

Don't blink or look away. You need to stay focused and keep at it as long as you can without staring.

One of three things will happen. About half the time the woman will simply not notice you. Don't stare obsessively at her (this is scary). Continue to walk and look for the next woman.

At the third attempt, she will fix the look on you but then will divert it. If this happens, you should do the same and continue to walk. However, in some cases, the woman will actually fix herself in your eyes and keep in touch with you. If this happens, don't react. Simply continue walking without changing your facial expression or pace.

Break eye contact when she does. In some cases she'll smile. If so, smile back, but if you're still looking, don't force yourself to smile first.

Keep in mind that, statistically, smiles are rewarded in about 85 percent of all cases. So if you feel like playing and have had enough eye contact, you can move on to the next level.

Smile first and make sure the statistics are true. Besides, it can be quite funny to make a woman smile just by passing next to her.

Never forget that this only applies to situations where you have already fixed your eyes on a woman and she hasn't deviated from it. For some reason she was intrigued and allowed herself to make eye contact with you.

This is a positive sign, so don't take it for granted! You've established a direct connection with her brain and emotions, and it's a perfect opportunity to make this emotion turn into something positive for her—all in a matter of seconds.

Eventually, if she comes in on a regular basis, she may become receptive enough to say hello when you two pass each other. Say hello back, but keep walking. Don't worry about what comes next. At the moment you're still practicing eye contact, so the pressure is off. After all, you didn't make any kind of breakthrough, just as she didn't, but you learned to make a connection.

Step 2—The Good Samaritan

Eye contact is one thing, conversation is another. If you feel intimidated by talking to beautiful women, try something completely innocent.

When you see a pretty woman, head to her and helpfully point to her, as if to say her shoelace seems loose or that she has something on her face—but keep walking.

All you have to do is hope she notices something that needs adjustment or correction, which makes you a Good Samaritan.

However, if everything seems perfect, invent something—tell her she has a bit of dirt on her face. Even if it's not true, her self-image will need a good furbishing, but she won't be upset because you were being a gentleman.

However, you gained experience, but not by appealing to beautiful women or addressing them in a lower way but by talking in a superior one—by provoking them a little and letting them think about themselves and what your intentions would be. In other words, you're acting like a dominant male, which, at least in the minds of these women, makes you a dominant male.

Do this several times, and you're on the right track to getting and maintaining the successful attitudes of an FA, which will guarantee you exactly the kind of woman you've always dreamed of.

Remember the three-second rule while being a Good Samaritan, and you will be surprised at how this simple trick will help your level of technique and confidence.

Step 3—The Praise

The praise works exactly the same way as the Good Samaritan, but this time you actually talk (as opposed to saying a few words) to the woman. Instead of arranging an excuse to tell her something, you will praise it.

This will not only make you talk with her, it will help you be more attentive, because, as always, you will only have three seconds to give a compliment, but it will make sense to this particular woman. Remember to continue without any kind of pressure to engage her.

While giving a compliment is harder than the Good Samaritan approach—you have no excuse to approach her and are putting yourself at risk by saying something positive about her—

you continue to practice the conversation with women, so it's okay to praise her, smile, and just keep walking.

However, as you evolve to reach this stage, you should set your personal goal to praise women followed by at least two questions. In other words, you're about to have a real conversation.

The key to this lies in asking the right questions. Never pose yes or no questions. Always ask something that leaves open the possibility of following up the conversation.

For example, if your opening cut is to praise her dress, ask her where she bought it and what it's material is. The more you know about the subject, the better, but don't go deep and try to be smarter than she is. It's still a simple conversation.

Step 4—Avoid Becoming a Friend

Having good visual contact, being a Good Samaritan, giving the right compliment, and having a casual and short conversation thanks to some well-timed questions are fine and good. But even after such a promising start, many men let their encounters degenerate into … the dangerous friend zone.

Being labeled as a friend in a woman's mind is like the kiss of death. Who needs another friend? There are ways to "rise from the dead" after becoming a friend, but it's much better to avoid it from the beginning than to have to resort to these advanced and treacherous techniques later.

Avoiding an unwanted friendship has everything to do with attitude—but since you're still a beginner, you probably don't have the ability to give off a certain sexual vibe. So you have to place the cards on the table as simply and directly as possible.

Once you've mastered step 3 and are comfortable with casual conversations with beautiful women, it's time to take control of these conversations. Of course, you won't make any kind of rude comment or ask something with no meaning; that would end the conversation. Instead, make that seemingly simple but at the same time treacherous question: "Are you the kind of person I should know?"

You can even ask from out of nowhere. Since this is your first conversation with her, the question is relevant, regardless of what you've said so far. The trick here is to catch the woman off-guard and remind her that however much your talk sounds innocent, there's a purpose to it.

You have just reminded her that it's not just a conversation being thrown out; it's a man and a woman getting to know each other. You gave her something to think about—sexual thoughts.

It's even better: the positions have now been reversed, and she is being evaluated rather than you. She probably isn't accustomed to something like that and will certainly make an effort to not lose points. In an unusual way, she will be able to answer no to your question, which will only bring you down.

However, as with any other answer, the obvious next question is "why?" You're now having the kind of conversations the FAs have.

TEN

Your House Is Your Love Nest

Women hate dirty, lazy, and uncaring men. So why let your house or apartment give you this impression about you? This is where you're going to bring women to have sex, so make sure your safe haven is prepared for love and that it projects the right image as soon as she enters. Otherwise, she'll turn around and run away—and not to your room.

Here are some hints:

Keep your home clean. Make sure the floor is clean, that your clothes are in the closet, and no trash is on display. Keep the temperature warm enough so the two of you can undress at will, but not so hot that you end up sweating a lot.

The bathroom is clean, right? A messy bathroom is no aphrodisiac, so make sure this is the neatest area of your home. The only things that should be in sight are quality cologne, shampoo, and other products that demonstrate your attention to detail.

Always have large, fluffy bath towels, two bathrobes, and an extra toothbrush still in the package. Also, having a few extra cushions is also a good idea. Remember to turn the phone off before you start having sex.

Dimmed lights are always a good idea. Other than that, have candles at hand. In fact, make sure you have a healthy storage of candles—they work as a powerful aphrodisiac.

Always have chocolate on hand and some white wine or champagne cooling in the fridge. Any kind of candy is good, but chocolate in particular is an excellent aphrodisiac. Although I don't recommend the use of alcohol, especially to "improve" your confidence or to soften a woman, alcohol at moderate levels is a classic and romantic thing. Never attempt to intentionally get a woman drunk—this is for rapists and not for flirting artists.

Make sure your house smells good. Aromatic candles are perfect for this, as they help create the ideal ambiance.

Have the appropriate music. Not anything too explicit. Instead, choose things like Enya, soundtracks, and other choices that please the female. Classical music is perfect, and these CDs are so cheap at most music stores that you can buy a copy to offer her as a reminder of the fantastic night you spent.

Contraceptives (condoms): keep them handy but out of sight, and know where they are. Keep some in various spaces of the house—you never know where the night goes.

ELEVEN

Simply Say Hello

For some of us, the best woman is the stranger we see every morning in the cafe or during a walk after work. If you're a dreamer, this is probably the woman for you—and the reason you bought this book.

I told you to bury that dream and start meeting other women—women you aren't so emotionally attached to—right now. For now, before you make her yours, I provide you with the way to approach your dreams. It's perfect for an initiate because you don't have to make a real move, not even show your dominant male side. All you need is a lot of consistency and persistence (hence the reason for being exclusively for beginners, or just for fun), but getting your foot in the door before making an initial move can be an asset.

While you're using this type of approach with the woman of your dreams, you will also be trying a more direct approach on dozens of other beautiful women. And you will be learning to satisfy them as only an experienced seducer knows.

So here's what you need to do. When you see a woman you like but can't get close to, make eye contact and say hello. Then smile, turn around, and continue doing what you were doing. When meeting her again (oh what a joy!), do the same thing.

Keep doing this whenever you see her. I assure you, by the third hello, she will be thinking about you. By the fifth hello, she'll wonder why you've never spoke to her. By the tenth hello, she'll be so intrigued, she'll start talking to you.

It will probably create questions about you, and she may even ask you directly why you've never advanced beyond a simple hello. Is there anything wrong with it? Do you know her from somewhere?

Always keep your answers vague and mysterious—after all, you've had twenty "dates," so she'll feel almost like you know her, even if you've just exchanged a single word.

From here you will have to start doing some work, but guess what—you're talking to the beautiful woman of your dreams, she is intrigued about you, and you made almost no effort and had no chance at embarrassment.

Of course, there are downsides in this type of approach. You can miss it, which can be particularly devastating if she's already begun to show interest in you. Or if you don't see her often (at least once a week), there's a strong possibility that your eye contact and smile may not be consistent enough to create an interest. And, finally, as it's obvious, this plan takes a long time to develop, and as an FA, you should like to measure the time of an achievement in minutes rather than months.

However, for a beginner, for a passionate CFS, or for a dominant male interested in entering the game of a long seduction just for enjoyment, the *hello approach* has no rivals.

Conclusion

You made it. Congratulations!

When you started reading this material, you probably didn't feel confident, didn't have high self-esteem, and didn't know how to deal with women. You might have felt like a loser.

You couldn't start a simple conversation with women, let alone imagine taking a beautiful one on a date. Sex? For you, maybe it was a distant dream.

In short, you were the typical CFS, a socially excluded man, and not the kind of guy who attracted the opposite sex. But, reaching the end of this book, learning the special tips and rules I've given you, and knowing more about women's dynamics, you're definitely not the same guy.

You can get close to a woman, interpret body signals, make eye contact, talk, get a date, and, of course, have sex. You are not intimidated by social status, by the level of beauty, or by the seemingly closed-off posture of a woman. You do your best and get the better of her.

You've evolved into an FA. You deal with women in such a natural, simple, and spontaneous way that you seem to have been born knowing how to do it.

I have taught you many valuable tips. For example, I've shown you that nightclubs are not the only place to meet women to have sex. You have learned that where there is an attractive woman (and a supportive background), there's a place for you to approach. And you also learned to break all that romantic and unrealistic vision while at the same time knowing how important this is within the female imagination.

We all live in a material world where money plays a very important part in our lives and of course all women think the same way in my opinion when it comes to this, and that is they all look for wealthy men but if you haven't got there yet, don't worry there are other things that can also go in your favor, make them feel loved, and play with them without being a d*ck, offer them something and make your dates fun for her and I promise you she will be yours.

If you have achieved good results using the methods and advices in this handbook (and I know you did), show it to a friend, a relative, or an acquaintance. If there's someone who needs to learn about what I have taught here, be sure to share this material.

Now, the world has one fewer CFS and one more FA who has confidence, strength, determination, and the ability to deal with all the dynamics of the game of conquest and love, giving women what they want and getting what they wish from women.

You're no longer a guy. You're a man.

www.ingramcontent.com/pod-product-compliance
Lightning Source LLC
Chambersburg PA
CBHW051558120626
46551CB00013B/1571